DARING AND DANGEROUS

SKY JUMPERS

JUDY GREENSPAN

Rourke
Educational Media

rourkeeducationalmedia.com

Before, During, and After Reading Activities

Before Reading: Building Background Knowledge and Academic Vocabulary

"Before Reading" strategies activate prior knowledge and set a purpose for reading. Before reading a book, it is important to tap into what your child or students already know about the topic. This will help them develop their vocabulary and increase their reading comprehension.

Questions and activities to build background knowledge:
1. *Look at the cover of the book. What will this book be about?*
2. *What do you already know about the topic?*
3. *Let's study the Table of Contents. What will you learn about in the book's chapters?*
4. *What would you like to learn about this topic? Do you think you might learn about it from this book? Why or why not?*

Building Academic Vocabulary
Building academic vocabulary is critical to understanding subject content.
Assist your child or students to gain meaning of the following vocabulary words.
Content Area Vocabulary
Read the list. What do these words mean?
- *atmosphere*
- *barge*
- *breakneck*
- *elite*
- *tandem*
- *veteran*

During Reading: Writing Component

"During Reading" strategies help to make connections, monitor understanding, generate questions, and stay focused.
1. *While reading, write in your reading journal any questions you have or anything you do not understand.*
2. *After completing each chapter, write a summary of the chapter in your reading journal.*
3. *While reading, make connections with the text and write them in your reading journal.*
   a) *Text to Self – What does this remind me of in my life? What were my feelings when I read this?*
   b) *Text to Text – What does this remind me of in another book I've read? How is this different from other books I've read?*
   c) *Text to World – What does this remind me of in the real world? Have I heard about this before? (News, current events, school, etc....)*

After Reading: Comprehension and Extension Activity

"After Reading" strategies provide an opportunity to summarize, question, reflect, discuss, and respond to text. After reading the book, work on the following questions with your child or students to check their level of reading comprehension and content mastery.
1. *Why do soldiers skydive in the military? (Summarize)*
2. *Why do people skydive for fun? (Infer)*
3. *How many skydivers were part of the biggest freefall formation in history? (Asking Questions)*
4. *What is the highest place you've jumped from? Do you want to jump from a plane? (Text to Self Connection)*

Extension Activity
Pick two of the amazing jumps mentioned in this book. With adult permission, search online to watch videos of the jumps. Now pretend you are a reporter and write a story about what you just saw. What words will you use to describe the jump? What do you want your reader to understand about the experience?

TABLE OF CONTENTS

BIGGEST,
HIGHEST, FASTEST

Skydivers open the airplane door. Listen to the wind howl. Look WAY down. And jump!

Georgia "Tiny" Broadwick

Georgia "Tiny" Broadwick was the first woman to parachute from an airplane. She was also the first woman to teach pilots how to parachute. Tiny jumped from airplanes more than 1,000 times and once landed on top of a moving train!

Hearts pounded when Luke Aikens took the plunge. The **veteran** skydiver had jumped thousands of times before. But this time, Luke wasn't wearing a parachute. He was aiming for a net!

☢ **veteran** (VET-ur-uhn): someone with a lot of experience

Record Setter

Bullseye! Luke hit the net and walked away. Calling his stunt, "Heaven Sent," he set a world record for the highest jump without a parachute.

Four hundred expert skydivers had two minutes to set a world record—and not die trying. Dropping at **breakneck** speed, 400 bodies fell into the largest freefall formation in history.

☢ **breakneck** (BRAKE-nek): extremely fast

Jumping from five airplanes over Udon, Thailand, skydivers held hands for a record-breaking 4.3 seconds.

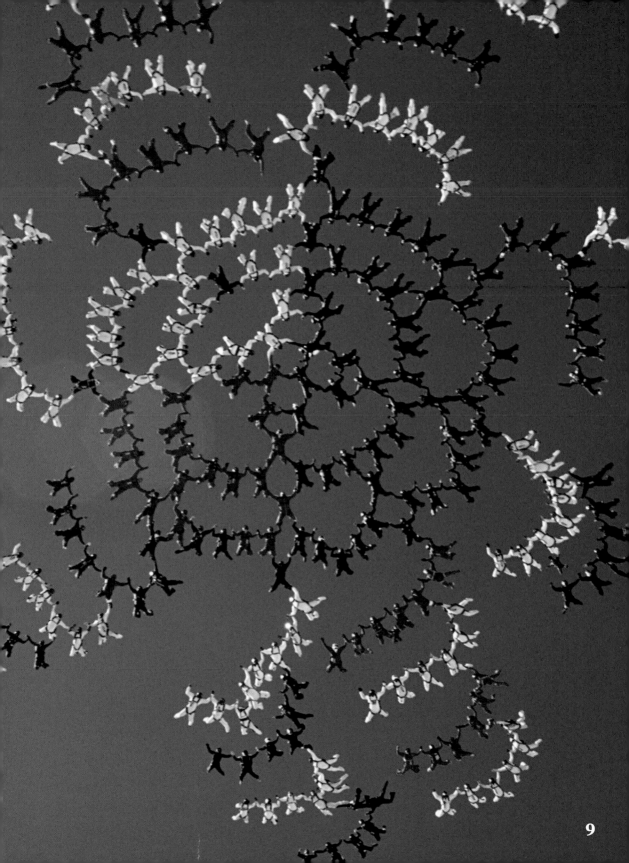

Freefalls are usually belly to Earth, or horizontal. But free-flyers go vertical for a death-defying drop!

Heading Down!

There's more air resistance to a belly-down fall because there is more surface area. Falling head first is the faster way to drop!

A hot air balloon lifted Alan Eustace 26 miles (42 kilometers) above Earth. Then, he cut loose from the balloon. Like a human rocket, Alan blasted through the **atmosphere**.

☢ **atmosphere** (AT-muhss-fihr): mixture of gases that surrounds a planet

Testing, Testing

Alan is not a stuntman. He's a computer scientist. He made the record-breaking jump to test a high-tech parachute and spacesuit.

THE ONLY
WAY IN

When wildfires rage and roads are blocked, the only way in is from the sky!

Smoke jumpers parachute in to fight the flames. Equipment, food, and water are dropped in too.

Flying in formation just inches apart, the Leap Frogs wow crowds. But this U.S. Navy parachute team doesn't just leap for fun. These **elite** military men perform daring rescue missions and parachute behind enemy lines.

☢ **elite** (ih-LEET): people with special skills or advantages

Some Navy SEALS have four legs and fur. Strapped to their two-legged partners, these courageous canines jump into action from thousands of feet up.

Paradogs

Once on the ground, military dogs sniff out hidden explosives or find enemy soldiers.

Why were beavers falling from the sky? Were they in the military too? Not quite. In 1948, beavers in Idaho were moved to another part of the state. Packed onto planes, crates of beavers were parachuted to their new homes.

DAREDEVIL STUNTS

Five skydivers wearing wingsuits once soared above New York's skyscrapers for two miles (3.2 kilometers) before parachuting to a **barge** in the Hudson River.

☢ **barge** (BARJ): a long boat with a flat bottom

Human Bats

A wingsuit is a one-piece suit with wings. Flying horizontally instead of falling straight down, wingsuiters stay in the air longer.

Who needs a plane when any towering perch will do? BASE jumpers launch from buildings, antennae, spans (bridges), and Earth (cliffs and other natural elevations). BASE jumping is one of the world's most dangerous sports.

First-time skydivers jump **tandem**, attached to an instructor. The youngest skydiver in history to jump tandem was only four years old. And in 2017, 102-year-old Kenny Meyer jumped for the first time!

 tandem (TAN-duhm): two things or people arranged one in front of the other

For expert skydivers, the sky's the limit. Some have BASE jumped from moving trucks, skydived from plane to plane, and jumped with their parachutes on fire!

MEMORY GAME

Can you match the image to what you read?

INDEX

SHOW WHAT YOU KNOW

1. What is a freefall?
2. What was Alan Eustace testing?
3. What do smoke jumpers do?
4. Who are the Leap Frogs?
5. Why are dogs in the military?

FURTHER READING

Goldish, Meish, *Skydiving Dogs (Dog Heroes)*, Bearport Publishing, 2014.

Mooney, Carla, *Skydiving (Sports to the Extreme)*, Rosen Central, 2015.

Paxton, Lionel, *Parachute Action Adventure for Kids: Paratroopers & Skydiving Heroes With Thrilling Parachute Pictures & Activities Book For Kids!*, LD Publications, 2013.

ABOUT THE AUTHOR

After researching this book, Judy Greenspan understands why so many people love to skydive. However, she isn't planning to try this thrilling sport herself. Judy prefers to leave an airplane after it lands!

Meet The Author!
www.meetREMauthors.com

www.rourkeeducationalmedia.com

PHOTO CREDITS: Cover and Title Pg ©joggiebotma; Pg 6, 8, 12, 16, 22, 27 ©Sergii Korolko; Pg 19 & 30 ©US Dept of Defense; Pg 17 & 30 ©U.S. Navy photo by Mass Communication Specialist 3rd Class Zachary Eshleman/Released; Pg 29 & 30 ©Mauricio Graiki; Pg 5 & 30 ©German-skydiver; Pg 15 & 30 ©US FOREST SERVICE; Pg 26 & 30 ©vuk8691; Pg 1 ©tobynabors; Pg 7 ©Radiomoscow; Pg 9 ©IPGGutenbergUKLtd; Pg 11 ©dzphotovideo; Pg 13 ©AleksandarGeorgiev; Pg 21 ©Tylinek; Pg 23 ©SindreEspejord; Pg 24 ©Wiki

Edited by: Keli Sipperley
Cover and Interior design by: Rhea Magaro-Wallace

Library of Congress PCN Data

Sky Jumpers / Judy Greenspan
(Daring and Dangerous)
ISBN 978-1-64369-073-5 (hard cover)
ISBN 978-1-64369-066-7 (soft cover)
ISBN 978-1-64369-216-6 (e-Book)
Library of Congress Control Number: 2018955856

Rourke Educational Media
Printed in the United States of America,
North Mankato, Minnesota